# Praise God With All Creation

### A Book of Prayer
### For Morning and Evening

Michael Kwatera, OSB

Resource Publications, Inc.
San Jose, California

Reprint Department
Resource Publications, Inc.
160 E. Virginia Street, #290
San Jose, CA 95112-5876
1-408-286-8505 (voice)
1-408-287-8748 (fax)

Library of Congress Cataloging-in-Publication Data
Kwatera, Michael.
   Praise God with all creation: a book of prayer for morning and evening / Michael Kwatera.
     p. cm.
   ISBN 0-89390-504-6 (pbk.)
    1. Catholic Church—Prayer-books and devotions—English. I. Title.
BX2130 .K93 2000
242'.082—dc21                             99-086151

Printed in the United States of America
00 01 02 03 04 | 5 4 3 2 1

Editorial director: Nick Wagner
Production coordinator: Mike Sagara
Copyeditor: Robin Witkin

For Joshua J. Jeide,
who delights in God's creation,
especially in horses, prairie dogs and marmots
and in the Wild West, their home and his.

# Contents

Introduction . . . . . . . . . . . . . . . . . . . . . . . 1

Sunday Morning . . . . . . . . . . . . . . . . . . . . 3

Sunday Evening . . . . . . . . . . . . . . . . . . . 7

Monday Morning . . . . . . . . . . . . . . . . . . . 11

Monday Evening. . . . . . . . . . . . . . . . . . . 15

Tuesday Morning . . . . . . . . . . . . . . . . . . . 19

Tuesday Evening . . . . . . . . . . . . . . . . . . . 23

Wednesday Morning. . . . . . . . . . . . . . . . . . 27

Wednesday Evening. . . . . . . . . . . . . . . . . . 31

Thursday Morning. . . . . . . . . . . . . . . . . . . 35

Thursday Evening. . . . . . . . . . . . . . . . . . . 39

Friday Morning . . . . . . . . . . . . . . . . . . . . 43

Friday Evening . . . . . . . . . . . . . . . . . . . . 49

Saturday Morning . . . . . . . . . . . . . . . . . . 53

Saturday Evening . . . . . . . . . . . . . . . . . . . 57

# Acknowledgments

The English translation of the Psalms and the Canticle of the Three Young Men is from the *Liturgical Psalter* © 1994, International Committee on English in the Liturgy, Inc. All rights reserved.

Scripture quotations (other than for the Psalms and the Canticle of the Three Young Men) are from the New Revised Standard Version of the Bible, copyright © 1989 by the Division of Christian Education of the National Council of Churches of Christ in the United States of America. Used by permission. All rights reserved.

The English translation of the letter of St. Clement from the *The Liturgy of the Hours* © 1974, International Committee on English in the Liturgy, Inc. (ICEL); the English translation of the Psalms and the Canticle of the Three Young Men from *The Liturgical Psalter* © 1995, ICEL. All rights reserved.

# Introduction

How did you first learn the biblical story of creation? I learned it from the illustrations of my Catholic grade school classmates that filled the narrow corkboard above the blackboard. Somehow those primitive drawings proclaimed the truth that the biblical writers polished over the centuries: the material creation is not God, but comes from God. Therefore it is good, not evil.

This book of prayers celebrates the same truth, a truth that rural people may know best of all. It is a truth that I have come to know better as the pastor of two rural parishes in central Minnesota.

The texts for each day of the week include the basic elements of the Liturgy of the Hours, the church's official prayer for morning and evening: a psalm, Scripture readings, intercessions, the Lord's Prayer, and a blessing.

In the morning, a brief reading from the Book of Genesis tells the creation story day by day as the Priestly tradition of the Hebrew Bible presents it. In the evening, a brief selection from a letter of St. Clement, first-century bishop of Rome, serves as commentary on the day's themes. Perhaps children would like to take the roles of "Storyteller" and "Preacher."

The psalms are taken from the *Liturgical Psalter*, a translation published by the International Commission on English in the Liturgy in 1994. The short lines of this version, which are like bursts of praise or petition, easily lend themselves to communal recitation by people of different ages.

Part of Psalm 104 is prayed each day at morning prayer from Sunday through Thursday and on Saturday. To some psalms or parts of a psalm are added lines from the Canticle of the Three Young Men from the Book of Daniel, chapter 3, which express similar themes or ideas. These lines from the canticle serve as a crescendo of praise that leads into the doxology ("Glory to the Father …").

The Scripture readings are taken from the New Revised Standard Version. The responses to the readings are drawn wholly or partially from the classic Divine Office hymns of the Benedictine tradition, in translations by Rev. Roger Schoenbechler, OSB, (1900–1986) of St. John's Abbey and the monks of Our Lady of Gethsemani Monastery. Father Roger's hymn texts appeared in *Book of Prayer* (St. John's Abbey Press, 1975) and deserve greater familiarity. I have presumed to change words or phrases here or there and to add several new verses of my own. Placed as they are after the Scripture readings, these hymn texts function a bit like the hymn in the classic Benedictine Office at Morning and Evening Prayer: as a kind of "theme song" for the time of day or hour of prayer. These hymns can be sung to the familiar tune OLD HUNDREDTH ("Praise God from Whom All Blessings Flow") or another tune of long metre (8.8.8.8). Of course they may be simply recited by all.

For the intercessions I have not included "ready to pray" petitions, but rather a list of groups of people and activities that should invite our prayer. I hope this will encourage intercessions to spring up in new ways and words from day to day depending on daily needs. The Lord's Prayer serves as a fitting summary and conclusion to the intercessions. A prayer (by the leader or by all) and a blessing bring the time of prayer to a close.

May this book help you and your family to worship the Maker of all things, the God who made us the new creation in Christ Jesus.

Michael Kwatera, OSB
May 15, 1999
Memorial of Sts. Isidore the Farmer
and Maria de la Cabeza

# Sunday Morning

Leader: How wonderful are your works, O Lord!

**All:      In wisdom you have made them all!**

Leader: All praise be yours, O Lord, through the light of heaven.

**All:      Glory and praise for ever!**

The Storyteller reads Genesis 1:1–5:

> In the beginning, when God created the heavens and the earth, the earth was a formless void and darkness covered the face of the deep, while a wind from God swept over the face of the waters. Then God said, "Let there be light"; and there was light. And God saw that the light was good; and God separated the light from the darkness. God called the light Day, and the darkness he called Night. And there was evening and morning, the first day.

## ■ Psalm 104:1–4
### Canticle of the Three Young Men (Dan 3:56,72,73)

Solo:   I will bless you, Lord my God!
        You fill the world with awe.
        You dress yourself in light,
        in rich, majestic light.

**All:      You stretched out the sky like a tent,
        built your house beyond the rain.
        You ride upon the clouds,
        the wind becomes your wings,
        the storm becomes your herald,
        your servants, bolts of light.**

Solo:   Bless God beyond the stars.

**All:**     **Give praise and glory.**

Solo:     Bless God, light and darkness.

**All:**     **Give praise and glory.**

Solo:     Bless God, lightning and clouds.

**All:**     **Give praise and glory.**

**All:**     **Glory to the Father, and to the Son,**
            **and to the Holy Spirit:**
            **as it was in the beginning, is now,**
            **and will be for ever. Amen.**

# ■ Scripture Reading: 2 Corinthians 4:5–6

Reader:  A reading from the second Letter of Saint Paul
            to the Corinthians.

            We do not proclaim ourselves; we proclaim Jesus
Christ as Lord and ourselves as your slaves for Jesus'
sake. For it is the God who said, "Let light shine out
of darkness," who has shown in our hearts to give
the light of the knowledge of the glory of God in the
face of Jesus Christ.

            The word of the Lord.

**All:**     **Thanks be to God.**

# ■ Silent Reflection

# ■ Response to the Reading

**All:**     **O gracious Maker, God of light,**
            **You gave us light that we might see**
            **The wonders of the world you made**
            **By your own will and wise decree.**

**We thank you for the sunlight bright,**
**Sustaining life and growth on earth.**
**We thank you for the light of grace**
**Which by your love gave us new birth.**

**Almighty Father, hear our cry**
**Through Jesus Christ, our Lord most high,**
**Whom in the Spirit we adore,**
**Who reigns with you forevermore. Amen.**

## ■ Intercessions

Leader: Jesus Christ is light from light, the Son of God who dispels the darkness of our hearts and minds. In his name let us pray for:

Our Family
Our Neighbors
Our Friends
Our Parishioners
Our Sisters and Brothers around the World

Let us pray as Christ, the King of all creation, has taught us:

**All:** **Our Father ....**

## ■ Prayer

By the leader or by all:

Lord God, source of heaven's glory,
be with us throughout this day
which you have made your own.
Fill us with your light in Jesus Christ,
so that we may see and love our world
as you do.
We ask this through the same Christ our Lord. Amen.

# ■ Blessing

Leader:  May the God of infinite goodness scatter the darkness of sin and brighten our hearts with holiness.

**All:**     **Amen.**

A sign of peace may be exchanged.

# Sunday Evening

Leader: How wonderful are your works, O Lord!

**All:** **In wisdom you have made them all!**

Leader: All praise be yours, O Lord, through the coming of darkness.

**All:** **Glory and praise for ever!**

The Preacher:

From a letter of Saint Clement, bishop of Rome:
Let us fix our gaze on the Father and Creator of the
whole world, and let us hold on to his peace and
blessing, his splendid and surpassing gifts. Let us
contemplate him in our thoughts and with our mind's
eye reflect upon the peaceful and restrained
unfolding of his plan; let us consider the care with
which he provides for the whole of his creation.

## ■ Psalm 139:1–3,7–12
## Canticle of the Three Young Men (Dan 3:56,71,72)

Solo: You search me, Lord, and you know me.
Wherever I sit or stand,
you read my inmost thoughts;
whenever I walk or rest,
you know where I have been.

**All:** **Where can I hide from you?**
**How can I escape your presence?**
**I scale the heavens, you are there!**
**I plunge to the depths, you are there!**

Solo: If I fly toward the dawn,
or settle across the sea,
even there you take hold of me,
your right hand directs me.

**All:** If I think night will hide me
and darkness give me cover,
I find darkness is not dark.
For you night shines like day,
darkness and light are one.

Solo: Bless God, beyond the stars.

**All:** Give praise and glory.

Solo: Bless God, night and day.

**All:** Give praise and glory.

Solo: Bless God, light and darkness.

**All:** Give praise and glory.

**All:** Glory to the Father, and to the Son,
and to the Holy Spirit:
as it was in the beginning, is now,
and will be for ever. Amen.

## ■ Scripture Reading: John 1:1–5

Reader: A reading from the Gospel according to John.

In the beginning was the Word, and the Word was
with God, and the Word was God. He was in the
beginning with God. All things came into being
through him, and without him not one thing came
into being. What has come into being in him was life,
and the life was the light of all people. The light
shines in the darkness, and the darkness did not
overcome it.

The Gospel of the Lord.

**All:** Praise to you, Lord Jesus Christ.

# ■ Silent Reflection

# ■ Response to the Reading

**All:**      **Divine Creator of the light**
         **Who bringing forth the golden ray,**
         **Did join the morning with the night**
         **And call the blessed union day.**

      **We bow to you whose mighty word**
         **Made time begin and heaven move;**
      **Lord, listen to our evening prayer,**
         **And warm us with the light of love.**

      **Almighty Father, hear our cry,**
         **Through Jesus Christ, our Lord most high,**
      **Whom in the Spirit we adore,**
         **Who reigns with you forevermore. Amen.**

# ■ Intercessions

Leader:  Our God is ever-watchful in night's darkness, and so we entrust to the Lord our:

      Work
      Learning
      Play
      Travel
      Activities
      Rest

      Let us give glory to the Father as Jesus, victor over death, has taught us:

**All:**      **Our Father ....**

## ■ Prayer

By the leader or by all:

> God of evening, God of night,
> darkness is never dark for you.
> Light our way
> in every dark time in our lives,
> in every dark place in our world.
> We ask this through Christ our Lord. Amen.

## ■ Blessing

Leader:  May the resurrection of Jesus be to us a source of blessing and life, both now and for ever.

**All:**     **Amen.**

A sign of peace may be exchanged.

# Monday Morning

Leader: How wonderful are your works, O Lord!

**All:**  **In wisdom you have made them all!**

Leader: All praise be yours, O Lord, through life-giving water.

**All:**  **Glory and praise for ever!**

The Storyteller reads from Genesis 1:6–8:

> God said: "Let there be a dome in the midst of the waters, and let it separate the waters from the waters." So God made the dome and separated the waters that were under the dome from the waters that were above the dome. And it was so. God called the dome Sky. And there was evening and there was morning, the second day.

## ■ Psalm 104:5–13
### Canticle of the Three Young Men (Dan 3:60,77,78)

Solo:  [Lord,] you made the earth solid,
fixed it for good.
You made the sea a cloak,
covering hills and all.

**All:**  **At your command
the sea fled your thunder,
swept over the mountains,
down the valleys to its place.
You set its limits,
never to drown the earth again.**

Solo:   You feed springs that feed brooks,
        rushing down ravines,
        water for wild beasts,
        for wild asses to drink.
        Birds nest nearby
        and sing among the leaves.

**All:**    **You drench the hills
        with rain from high heaven.
        You nourish the earth
        with what you create.**

Solo:   Bless God, waters above.

**All:**    **Give praise and glory.**

Solo:   Bless God, fountains and springs.

**All:**    **Give praise and glory.**

Solo:   Bless God, rivers and seas.

**All:**    **Give praise and glory.**

**All:**    **Glory to the Father, and to the Son,
        and to the Holy Spirit:
        as it was in the beginning, is now,
        and will be for ever. Amen.**

## ■ Scripture Reading: Job 38:8–11,16

Reader:  A reading from the Book of Job.

The LORD answered Job out of the whirlwind: "Who shut in the sea with doors when it burst out from the womb?—when I made the clouds its garment, and thick darkness its swaddling band, and prescribed bounds for it, and set bars and doors, and said, 'Thus far shall you come, and no farther, and here shall your proud waves be stopped'? Have you entered into the springs of the sea, or walked in the recesses of the deep?"

The word of the Lord.

**All:** **Thanks be to God.**

# ■ Silent Reflection

# ■ Response to the Reading

**All:** **O boundless Maker of the skies,**
**The earth and sky you did divide,**
**Then put the waters in their place,**
**They now in sky and earth abide.**

**The rainclouds hover overhead,**
**The heat of sun burns hot and bright,**
**But with the rivers, seas, and lakes,**
**You keep the earth from drought and blight.**

**Almighty Father, hear our cry,**
**Through Jesus Christ, our Lord most high,**
**Whom in the Spirit we adore,**
**Who reigns with you forevermore. Amen.**

# ■ Intercessions

Leader: Let us draw deeply from the springs of God's mercy as we pray for:

All Christians
Nations and Peoples
Those who suffer from illness and injury
Those who lack food, shelter and clothing
Those who have died

Remembering God's love and care for us, let us pray in the words of Jesus our brother:

**All:** **Our Father ....**

# ■ Prayer

By the leader or by all:

> Let your saving love, O God,
> be a life-giving stream
> for body, soul, and spirit.
> Rain down your grace
> on the dry, dusty places of our lives,
> and refresh us with your living water
> in Jesus Christ.
> We ask this through the same Christ our Lord. Amen.

# ■ Blessing

Leader: May Christ bless us with his loving presence and his word of truth.

**All:** **Amen.**

A sign of peace may be exchanged.

# Monday Evening

Leader: How wonderful are your works, O Lord!

**All:    In wisdom you have made them all!**

Leader: All praise be yours, O Lord, through sky above.

**All:    Glory and praise for ever!**

The Preacher:

> From a letter of Saint Clement, bishop of Rome:
> By God's direction the heavens are in motion, and
> they are subject to him in peace. Day and night fulfill
> the course he has established without interfering with
> each other.
>
> Yet unexplored regions of the abysses and
> inexpressible realms of the deep are subject to his
> laws. The mass of the boundless sea, joined together
> by his ordinance in a single expanse, does not
> overflow its prescribed limits but flows as he
> commanded it.

## ■ Psalm 33:1–9
### Canticle of the Three Young Men (Dan 3:59,64,65)

Solo:    Shout joy to the Lord,
            lovers of justice,
            how right to praise!
            Praise God on the harp,
            with ten-stringed lyre
            sing to the Lord.

**All:    Sing God a new song,
            Play music to match
            your shout of joy.**

Solo:   For the word of the Lord is true:
        what God says, God does.
        This lover of truth and justice
        fills the earth with love.

**All:**    **God speaks: the heavens are made;**
        **God breathes: the stars shine.**
        **God bottles the waters of the sea**
        **and stores them in the deep.**

Solo:   All earth, be astounded,
        stand in awe of God.
        God speaks: the world is;
        God commands: all things appear.

Solo:   Bless God, highest heavens.

**All:**    **Give praise and glory.**

Solo:   Bless God, rainstorm and dew.

**All:**    **Give praise and glory.**

Solo:   Bless God, gales and winds.

**All:**    **Give praise and glory.**

**All:**    **Glory to the Father, and to the Son,**
        **and to the Holy Spirit:**
        **as it was in the beginning, is now,**
        **and will be for ever. Amen.**

## ■ Scripture Reading: Isaiah 55:10–11

Reader: A reading from the Book of the Prophet Isaiah.

For as the rain and snow come down from heaven
and do not return there until they have watered the
earth, making it bring forth and sprout, giving seed to
the sower and bread to the eater, so shall my word
be that goes out from my mouth; it shall not return to
me empty, but it shall accomplish that which I
purpose, and succeed in the thing for which I sent it.

The word of the Lord.

**All:**  **Thanks be to God.**

## ■ Silent Reflection

## ■ Response to the Reading

**All:**  **O boundless Maker of the sky,**
**You raise the fertile clouds on high,**
**And bless the earth with flowing streams,**
**To quicken every living thing.**

**O let your gentle grace be poured**
**Like rain upon us, loving Lord.**
**Drink from above for thirsty hearts**
**To all in need your love imparts.**

**Almighty Father, hear our cry,**
**Through Jesus Christ, our Lord most high,**
**Whom in the Spirit we adore,**
**Who reigns with you forevermore. Amen.**

## ■ Intercessions

Leader: God has told us that the prayer of the lowly pierces the heavens, so we confidently ask God to care for:

Our Church
Our World
Our Nation
Our Community
Ourselves

In the words Jesus gave us, let us pray for all in need:

**All:**  **Our Father ....**

## ■ Prayer

By the leader or by all:

Wider and higher than the sky, O God,
is your love for us and for all people.
Protect us as we follow your Son, Jesus Christ,
who went up to heaven
and prepares for us
a place of life and glory,
for ever and ever. Amen.

## ■ Blessing

Leader: May God direct our steps and show us how to live in
love and peace.

**All:** **Amen.**

A sign of peace may be exchanged.

# Tuesday Morning

Leader: How wonderful are your works, O Lord!

**All:  In wisdom you have made them all!**

Solo:  All praise be yours, O Lord, through all that grows.

**All:  Glory and praise for ever!**

The Storyteller reads Genesis 1:9–13:

> God said: "Let the waters under the sky be gathered together in one place, and let the dry land appear." And it was so. God called the dry land Earth, and the waters that were gathered together he called Seas. And God saw that it was good. Then God said, "Let the earth put forth vegetation: plants yielding seed, and fruit trees of every kind on earth that bear fruit with the seed in it." And it was so. The earth brought forth vegetation: plants yielding seed of every kind, and trees of every kind bearing fruit with the seed in it. And God saw that it was good. And there was evening and there was morning, the third day.

## ■ Psalm 104:13–18
### Canticle of the Three Young Men (Dan 3:76)

Solo:  [Lord,] you nourish the earth
with what you create.

**All:  You make grass grow for the cattle,
make plants grow for people,
food to eat from the earth
and wine to warm the heart,
oil to glisten on faces
and bread for bodily strength.**

Solo:    In Lebanon God planted trees,
the flourishing cedar.
Sparrows nest in the branches,
the stork in treetops.
High crags for wild goats,
rock holes for badgers.

Solo:    Bless God, trees and plants.

**All:**    **Give praise and glory.**

Solo:    Bless God, seedtime and harvest.

**All:**    **Give praise and glory.**

Solo:    Bless God, fields and crops.

**All:**    **Give praise and glory.**

**Glory to the Father, and to the Son,
and to the Holy Spirit:
as it was in the beginning, is now,
and will be for ever. Amen.**

## ■ Scripture Reading: Mark 5:26–29

Reader:  A reading from the Gospel according to Mark.

Jesus said: "This is how it is with the kingdom of God; it is as if a man were to scatter seed on the land and would sleep and rise night and day and the seed would sprout and grow, he knows not how. Of its own accord the land yields fruit, first the blade, then the ear, then the full grain in the ear. And when the grain is ripe, he wields the sickle at once, for the harvest has come."

The Gospel of the Lord.

**All:**    **Praise to you, Lord Jesus Christ.**

# ■ Silent Reflection

# ■ Response to the Reading

All: Kind Maker of the earth's great sphere,
You made the fertile soil appear
By gath'ring waters into seas,
Providing land for plants and trees.

You made the earth bring forth new seeds,
With fruits and grains for all our needs,
Let fruitful harvests multiply,
The needs of all to satisfy.

Almighty Father, hear our cry,
Through Jesus Christ, our Lord most high,
Whom in the Spirit we adore,
Who reigns with you forevermore. Amen.

# ■ Intercessions

Leader: Just as God makes a garden spring up, so will justice
and praise spring up before all the nations in answer
to our prayers. Let us remember:

Our Family
Our Neighbors
Our Friends
Our Parishioners
Our Sisters and Brothers around the World

Let us ask for our daily bread as Jesus taught us:

All: Our Father ....

# ■ Prayer

By the leader or by all:

> Lord God, sower of blessing,
> all growing things offer you
> a silent hymn of praise.
> Let the words and deeds we sow this day
> bring forth an abundant harvest of goodness
> for us and for others,
> both now and for ever. Amen.

# ■ Blessing

Leader: May the only-begotten Son of God bless us and assist us in all our needs.

**All:    Amen.**

A sign of peace may be exchanged.

# Tuesday Evening

Leader: How wonderful are your works, O Lord!

**All:** **In wisdom you have made them all!**

Leader: All praise be yours, O Lord, through fertile land.

**All:** **Glory and praise for ever!**

The Preacher:

> From a letter of Saint Clement, bishop of Rome:
> By God's will the earth blossoms in the proper
> seasons and produces abundant food for people
> and animals and all the living things on it without
> reluctance and without any violation of what he
> has arranged.

## ■ Psalm 67

Solo: Favor and bless us, Lord.
Let your face shine on us,
revealing your way to all peoples,
salvation the world over.

**All:** **Let nations sing your praise,**
**every nation on earth.**

Solo: The world will shout for joy,
for you rule the planet with justice.
In fairness you govern the nations
and guide the peoples of earth.

**All:** **Let nations sing your praise,**
**every nation on earth.**

Solo: The land delivers its harvest,
God, our God, has blessed us.
O God, continue your blessing,
may the whole world worship you.

**All:** Glory to the Father, and to the Son,
and to the Holy Spirit:
as it was in the beginning, is now,
and will be for ever. Amen.

## ■ Scripture Reading: Matthew 6:25,28b–30

Reader: A reading from the Gospel according to Matthew.

Jesus said: "Therefore I tell you, do not worry about
your life, what you will eat or what you will drink, or
about your body, what you will wear. Is not life
more than food, and the body more than clothing?
Consider the lilies of the field, how they grow; they
neither toil nor spin, yet I tell you, even Solomon in
all his glory was not clothed like one of these. But if
God so clothes the grass of the field, which is alive
today and tomorrow is thrown into the oven, will he
not much more clothe you—you of little faith?"

The Gospel of the Lord.

**All:** Praise to you, Lord Jesus Christ.

## ■ Silent Reflection

## ■ Response to the Reading

**All:** Great God, we sing that mighty hand
By which supported still we stand
The op'ning day your mercy shows,
That mercy crowns it till its close.

By day, by night, at home, abroad,
Still we are guarded by our God:
By God's enduring bounty fed,
By God's unfailing counsel led.

**Almighty Father, hear our cry,**
  **Through Jesus Christ, our Lord most high,**
**Whom in the Spirit we adore,**
**Who reigns with you forevermore. Amen.**

# ■ Intercessions

Leader: How great is your name, O Lord our God, through all the earth! We call upon your name as we ask your help in our

Work
Learning
Play
Travel
Activities

Let us place all our confidence in God as we pray the Lord's Prayer:

**All:** **Our Father ....**

# ■ Prayer

By the leader or by all:

Lord of the harvest,
your Son sows the seed of your Word
within our hearts.
Make us good and fertile soil,
eager to hear your message
with faith and understanding,
and ready to do what you ask of us.
We make this prayer through Christ our Lord. Amen.

# ■ Blessing

Leader:  May the peace of Christ live always in our hearts and
in our home.

**All:**     **Amen.**

A sign of peace may be exchanged.

# Wednesday Morning

Leader:  How wonderful are your works, O Lord!

**All:**     **In wisdom you have made them all!**

Leader:  All praise be yours, O Lord, through golden sun.

**All:**     **Glory and praise for ever!**

The Storyteller reads Genesis 1:14–19:

> God said: "Let there be lights in the dome of the sky to separate the day from the night; and let them be for signs and for seasons and for days and years, and let them be lights in the dome of the sky to give light upon the earth." And it was so. God made the two great lights—the greater light to rule the day and the lesser light to rule the night—and the stars. God set them in the dome of the sky to give light upon the earth, to rule over the day and over the night, and to separate the light from the darkness. And God saw that it was good. And there was evening and there was morning, the fourth day.

## ■ Psalm 19:1–7
### Canticle of the Three Young Men (Dan 3:62,66)

Solo:    The sky tells the glory of God,
         tells the genius of God's work.

**All:**     **Day carries the news to day,**
         **night brings the message to night,**
         **without a word, without a sound,**
         **without a voice being heard,**
         **yet their message fills the world,**
         **their news reaches its rim.**

Solo:      There God has pitched a tent
               for the sun to rest and rise renewed
               like a bridegroom rising from bed,
               an athlete eager to run the race.

All:      **It springs from the edge of the earth,
               runs a course across the sky,
               to win the race at heaven's end.
               Nothing on earth escapes its heat.**

Solo:      Bless God, sun and moon.

All:      **Give praise and glory.**

Solo:      Bless God, fire and heat.

All:      **Give praise and glory.**

Solo:      Bless God, cold and warmth.

All:      **Give praise and glory.**

All:      **Glory to the Father, and to the Son,
               and to the Holy Spirit:
               as it was in the beginning, is now,
               and will be for ever. Amen.**

## ■ Scripture Reading: Sirach 42:16; 43:1–5

Reader:   A reading from the Book of Sirach.

The sun looks down on everything with its light, and the work of the Lord is full of his glory.

The pride of the higher realms is the clear vault of the sky, as glorious to behold as the sight of the heavens. The sun, when it appears, proclaims as it rises what a marvelous instrument it is, the work of the Most High. At noon it parches the land, and who can withstand its burning heat? A man tending a furnace works in burning heat, but three times as hot is the sun scorching the mountains; it breathes out fiery vapors, and its bright rays blind the eyes. Great is the Lord who made it; at his orders it hurries on its course.

The word of the Lord.

**All:**     **Thanks be to God.**

# ■ Silent Reflection

# ■ Response to the Reading

**All:**     **O God, your hand once spread the sky**
             **And all its shining stars on high.**
          **You, when the fourth day was begun,**
             **Did frame the circle of the sun.**

          **O shine your light upon our mind;**
             **All darksome guilt of sin unbind.**
          **Direct us in the way of right,**
             **As children filled with your true light.**

          **Almighty Father, hear our cry**
             **Through Jesus Christ, our Lord most high,**
          **Whom in the Spirit we adore,**
             **Who reigns with you forevermore. Amen.**

# ■ Intercessions

Leader:  May our prayers be like the sun's light and warmth for all in need. Let us remember:

         All Christians
         Nations and Peoples
         Those who suffer from illness and injury
         Those who lack food, shelter, and clothing
         Those who have died

         Mindful of all these people, let us pray as Jesus taught us:

**All:**     **Our Father ....**

## ■ Prayer

By the leader or by all:

> Bright is your sun, O God,
> a strong ruler for the day,
> but even stronger is your love for us.
> Gladden us with your heavenly light
> in Jesus Christ,
> the sun that knows no setting.
> He lives and reigns as Lord for ever and ever. Amen.

## ■ Blessing

Leader:  May Christ grant us a share of his life and light, both now and for ever.

**All:**      **Amen.**

A sign of peace may be exchanged.

# Wednesday Evening

Leader: How wonderful are your works, O Lord!

**All:** **In wisdom you have made them all.**

Leader: All praise be yours, O Lord, through moon and stars.

**All:** **Glory and praise for ever!**

The Preacher:

> From a letter of Saint Clement, bishop of Rome:
> Consider, beloved, how the Lord keeps reminding us
> of the resurrection that is to come, of which he has
> made the Lord Jesus Christ the firstfruits by raising
> him from the dead. Let us look, beloved, at the
> resurrection that occurs at its appointed time. Day
> and night show us a resurrection; the night lies in
> sleep, day rises again; the day departs, night takes
> its place.

## ■ Psalm 121

Solo: If I look to the mountains,
will they come to my aid?
My help is from the Lord,
who made earth and the heavens.

**All:** **May God, ever watchful,**
**keep you from stumbling;**
**the guardian of Israel**
**neither rests nor sleeps.**

Solo: God shields you,
a protector by your side.
The sun shall not harm you by day
nor the moon by night.

**All:**     God shelters you from evil,
             securing your life.
             God watches over you near and far,
             now and always.

**All:**     Glory to the Father, and to the Son,
             and to the Holy Spirit:
             as it was in the beginning, is now,
             and will be for ever. Amen.

## ■ Scripture Reading: Sirach 43:6–10

Reader: A reading from the Book of Sirach.

> It is the moon that marks the changing seasons,
> governing the times, their everlasting sign. From the
> moon comes the sign for the festal days, a light that
> wanes when it completes its course. The new moon,
> as its name suggests, renews itself; how marvelous it
> is in this change, a beacon to the hosts on high,
> shining in the vault of the heavens!
>      The glory of the stars is the beauty of heaven, a
> glittering array in the heights of the Lord. On the
> orders of the Holy One they stand in their appointed
> places; they never relax in their watches.

The word of the Lord.

**All:**     **Thanks be to God.**

## ■ Silent Reflection

# ■ Response to the Reading

**All:**   O God, you hold all things in space,
Each star and planet in its place,
The days and years are your design,
Each change of season you define.

As we life's eventide draw near,
Give us your light, remove our fear,
With happy death may we be blest,
And find in you eternal rest.

Almighty Father, hear our cry,
Through Jesus Christ, our Lord most high,
Whom in the Spirit we adore,
Who reigns with you forevermore. Amen.

# ■ Intercessions

Leader:  We are to shine on the world like bright stars, giving
it the light of life by our prayers. Let us ask God's
blessing on:

Our Church
Our World
Our Nation
Our Community
Ourselves

In the words Jesus gave us, let us pray to share the
life of God's reign:

**All:**   **Our Father ....**

## ■ Prayer

By the leader or by all:

> Shine in our darkness, O God,
> as the moon brightens the way
> for mortals and animals.
> As day turns into night,
> turn away from us all evil and harm
> with the power of your Son, Jesus Christ.
> A strong savior is he, for ever and ever. Amen.

## ■ Blessing

Leader: May the Lord who is faithful guard us from evil and strengthen us in the ways of peace.

**All:**    **Amen.**

A sign of peace may be exchanged.

# Thursday Morning

Leader: How wonderful are your works, O Lord!

**All:**     **In wisdom you have made them all!**

Leader: All praise be yours, O Lord, through all that swims.

**All:**     **Glory and praise for ever!**

The Storyteller reads Genesis 1:20–23:

> God said: "Let the waters bring forth swarms of living creatures, and let birds fly above the earth across the dome of the sky." So God created the great sea monsters and every living creature that moves, of every kind, with which the waters swarm, and every winged bird of every kind. And God saw that it was good. God blessed them, saying, "Be fruitful and multiply and fill the waters in the seas, and let birds multiply on the earth." And there was evening and there was morning, the fifth day.

## ■ Psalm 104:24–26
### Canticle of the Three Young Men (Dan 3:74,79)

Solo:     God, how fertile your genius!
You shape each thing,
you fill the world
with what you do.

**All:**     **I watch the sea, wide and deep,
filled with fish, large and small,
with ships that ply their trade,
and your toy, Leviathan.***

Solo:     Bless God, earth and sea.

**All:**     **Give praise and glory.**

*A mythical sea monster.

Solo:   Bless God, fishes and whales.

**All:**   **Give praise and glory.**

Solo:   Bless God, creatures that move in the waters.

**All:**   **Give praise and glory.**

**All:**   **Glory to the Father, and to the Son,**
**and to the Holy Spirit:**
**as it was in the beginning, is now,**
**and will be for ever. Amen.**

## ■ Scripture Reading: Sirach 43:24–26

Reader:  A reading from the Book of Sirach.

By his plan [God] stilled the deep and planted islands in it. Those who sail the sea tell of its dangers, and we marvel at what we hear. In it are strange and marvelous creatures, all kinds of living things, and huge sea-monsters. Because of him each of his messengers succeeds, and by his word all things hold together.

The word of the Lord.

**All:**   **Thanks be to God.**

## ■ Silent Reflection

## ■ Response to the Reading

**All:**   **O God of might and power great,**
**Creation does your Word await:**
**"Let there be creatures in the seas!**
**Let others fly on high with ease!"**

**Thus fishes swim in waters deep**
**And birds their flight in air do keep;**
**The earth with life you wisely fill,**
**Air, land, and sea, each by your will.**

> **Almighty Father, hear our cry,**
> **Through Jesus Christ, our Lord most high,**
> **Whom in the Spirit we adore,**
> **Who reigns with you forevermore. Amen.**

# ■ Intercessions

Leader: Let us call upon our God, who is an ocean-depth of mercy, and pray for:

> Our Family
> Our Neighbors
> Our Friends
> Our Parishioners
> Our Sisters and Brothers around the World

Let us pray as Christ the Lord has taught us:

**All:** **Our Father ....**

# ■ Prayer

By the leader or by all:

> Ever-living God,
> as little fishes are born in the water,
> so we Christians are born in the waters of baptism.
> Renew in us
> the grace of being your children,
> united with you in Jesus Christ,
> through the Holy Spirit,
> for ever and ever. Amen.

# ■ Blessing

Leader: May God make us steadfast in faith, joyful in hope, and untiring in love all the days of our life.

**All: Amen.**

A sign of peace may be exchanged.

# Thursday Evening

Leader: How wonderful are your works, O Lord!

**All:** **In wisdom you have made them all!**

Leader: All praise be yours, O Lord, through all that flies.

**All:** **Glory and praise for ever!**

The Preacher:

From a letter of Saint Clement, bishop of Rome:
The seasons, spring, summer, autumn and winter,
follow one another in harmony. The quarters from
which the winds blow function in due season
without the least deviation. And the ever-flowing
springs, created for our health as well as our
enjoyment, unfailingly ... sustain human life. The
tiniest of living creatures meet together in harmony
and peace.

## ■ Psalm 104:10,12,17
### Canticle of the Three Young Men (Dan 3:80)

Solo: [Lord,] you feed springs that feed brooks,
rushing down ravines.
Birds nest nearby
and sing among the leaves.

**All:** **In Lebanon God planted trees,**
**the flourishing cedar.**
**Sparrows nest in the branches,**
**the stork in treetops.**

Solo: Bless God, birds of the air.

**All:** **Give praise and glory.**

Solo: Bless God, every kind of bird.

**All:** **Give praise and glory.**

Solo: Bless God, creatures that fly.

**All:** **Give praise and glory.**

**All:** **Glory to the Father, and to the Son,
and to the Holy Spirit:
as it was in the beginning, is now,
and will be for ever. Amen.**

## ■ Scripture Reading: Matthew 6:25–26

Reader: A reading from the Gospel according to Matthew.

Jesus said: "Therefore I tell you, do not worry about your life, what you will eat or what you will drink, or about your body, what you will wear. Is not life more than food, and the body more than clothing? Look at the birds of the air; they neither sow nor reap nor gather into barns, and yet your heavenly Father feeds them. Are you not of more value than they?"

The Gospel of the Lord.

**All:** **Praise to you, Lord Jesus Christ.**

## ■ Silent Reflection

## ■ Response to the Reading

**All:** **O bounteous Maker of all life,
You saw the empty depth and height,
And filled them with the living things
Which swim by fins and fly on wings.**

**In all that moves through seas and air
Great is your glory, bright and fair.
To you, their Lord, we voice our praise:
How lovely are your works and ways!**

**Almighty Father, hear our cry,**
**Through Jesus Christ, our Lord most high,**
**Whom in the Spirit we adore,**
**Who reigns with you forevermore. Amen.**

## ■ Intercessions

Leader: Like a soaring eagle, God sees our needs even before
we ask. But let us pray for God's blessing in our

Work
Learning
Play
Travel
Activities

Let us place all our trust in God as we pray the Lord's
Prayer:

**All:** **Our Father ....**

## ■ Prayer

By the leader or by all:

With all that has wings—
with birds and bugs,
with bats and bees and butterflies—
we lift our praise above, Lord God.
Let our prayers reach you in highest heaven,
where angels worship you night and day,
for ever and ever. Amen.

## ■ Blessing

Leader: May the peace of Christ remain with us always.

**All:** **Amen.**

A sign of peace may be exchanged.

# Friday Morning

Leader: How wonderful are your works, O Lord!

**All:     In wisdom you have made them all!**

Leader: All praise be yours, O Lord, through all creatures on earth.

**All:     Glory and praise for ever!**

The Storyteller reads from Genesis 1:24–27:

> God said: "Let the earth bring forth living creatures of every kind; cattle and creeping things and wild animals of the earth of every kind." And it was so. God made the wild animals of the earth of every kind, and the cattle of every kind, and everything that creeps upon the ground of every kind. And God saw that it was good.

> Then God said, "Let us make humankind in our image, according to our likeness; and let them have dominion over the fish of the sea, and over the birds of the air, and over the cattle, and over all the wild animals of the earth, and over every creeping thing that creeps upon the earth."

> So God created humankind in his image, in the image of God he created them; male and female he created them.

## ■ Psalm 144:12–15
### Canticle of the Three Young Men (Dan 3:81,82)

Solo:    God, you shape our sons
like tall, sturdy plants;
you sculpt our daughters
like pillars for a palace.

All:     **You fill our barns
with all kinds of food,
you bless our fields
with sheep by the thousands
and fatten all our cattle.**

Solo:    There is no breach in the walls,
no outcry in the streets, no exile.
We are a people blest with these gifts,
blest with the Lord as our God!

Solo:    Bless God, beasts of the earth.

All:     **Give praise and glory.**

Solo:    Bless God, wild animals and tame.

All:     **Give praise and glory.**

Solo:    Bless God, all humankind.

All:     **Give praise and glory.**

All:     **Glory to the Father, and to the Son,
and to the Holy Spirit:
as it was in the beginning, is now,
and will be for ever. Amen.**

or:

# ■ Psalm 104:19–23,27–34,35b
## Canticle of the Three Young Men (Dan 3:81,82)

Solo:    [God,] your moon knows when to rise,
your sun when to set.
Your darkness brings on night
when wild beasts prowl.
The young lions roar to you
in search of prey.

All:    **They slink off to dens**
**to rest at daybreak,**
**then people rise to work**
**until the daylight fades.**

Solo:   Bless God, beasts of the earth.

All:    **Give praise and glory.**

Solo:   Bless God, wild animals and tame.

All:    **Give praise and glory.**

Solo:   Bless God, all humankind.

All:    **Give praise and glory.**

All:    **Glory to the Father, and to the Son,**
**and to the Holy Spirit:**
**as it was in the beginning, is now,**
**and will be for ever. Amen.**

# ■ Scripture Reading: Sirach 42:21–25

Reader:  A reading from the Book of Sirach.

[The Most High] has set in order the splendor of his wisdom; he is from all eternity one and the same. Nothing can be added or taken away, and he needs no one to be his counselor. How desirable are all his works, and how sparkling they are to see! All things live and remain forever; each creature is preserved to meet a particular need. All things come in pairs, one opposite the other, and he has made nothing incomplete. Each supplements the virtues of the other. Who could ever tire of seeing his glory?

The word of the Lord.

All:    **Thanks be to God.**

# ■ Silent Reflection

# ■ Response to the Reading

All:  O God of all the earth's wide span
The world you did most wisely plan!
You ordered that the earth should bear
Each type of beast and our first pair.

All living things, by your command,
Receive their life from your own hand
So that, as seasons come and go,
They might assist us here below.

Almighty Father, hear our cry,
Through Jesus Christ, our Lord most high,
Whom in the Spirit we adore,
Who reigns with you forevermore. Amen.

# ■ Intercessions

Leader:  We are creatures of earth, but our true home is in
heaven with our Creator. Let us ask God, the Maker
of heaven and earth, to remember:

All Christians
Nations and Peoples
Those who suffer from illness and injury
Those who lack food, shelter, and clothing
Those who have died

Let us pray to our heavenly Father as Jesus taught us:

**All: Our Father ....**

# ■ Prayer

By the leader or by all:

> Glory to you, Lord God,
> for all that you have made!
> Help us to care for all animals and plants,
> so that we may use wisely
> the creatures that come generously
> from your hand.
> Glory to you, Lord God,
> glory to you,
> both now and for ever. Amen.

# ■ Blessing

Leader: May God the Father and the Lord Jesus Christ grant peace, love, and faith to all of us.

**All:**      **Amen.**

A sign of peace may be exchanged.

# Friday Evening

Leader: How wonderful are your works, O Lord!

**All:** **In wisdom you have made them all!**

Leader: All praise be yours, O Lord, through humankind, the crown of all creation.

**All:** **Glory and praise for ever!**

The Preacher:

> From a letter of Saint Clement, bishop of Rome:
> Let us then approach [God] in holiness of soul,
> raising up to him hands pure and undefiled, out of
> love for our good and merciful Father who has made
> us a chosen portion for himself.

## ■ Psalm 8

Solo: Lord our God,
the whole world tells
the greatness of your name.
Your glory reaches
beyond the stars.

**All:** **Even the babble of infants
declares your strength,
your power to halt
the enemy and avenger.**

Solo: I see your handiwork
in the heavens:
the moon and the stars
you set in place.

All: **What is humankind**
**that you remember them,**
**the human race**
**that you care for them?**

Solo: You treat them like gods,
dressing them in glory and splendor.
You give them charge of the earth,
laying all at their feet:

All: **Cattle and sheep,**
**wild beasts,**
**birds of the sky,**
**fish of the sea,**
**every swimming creature.**

Solo: Lord our God,
the whole world tells
the greatness of your name.

All: **Glory to the Father, and to the Son,**
**and to the Holy Spirit:**
**as it was in the beginning, is now,**
**and will be for ever. Amen.**

## ■ Scripture Reading: 1 Corinthians 15:45–49

Reader: A reading from the first Letter of Saint Paul
to the Corinthians.

Thus it is written: "The first man, Adam, became a
living being"; the last Adam became a life-giving
spirit. But it is not the spiritual that is first, but the
physical, and then the spiritual. The first man was
from earth, a man of dust; the second man is from
heaven. As was the man of dust, so are those who
are of the dust; as is the man of heaven, so are those
who are of heaven. Just as we have borne the image
of the man of dust, we will also bear the image of
the man of heaven.

The word of the Lord.

**All:    Thanks be to God.**

# ■ Silent Reflection

# ■ Response to the Reading

**All:    Creation is your work of love,
            You rule the world by wise decrees,
            We therefore come before you, Lord,
            To place before you all our pleas.**

**Your pardon for our sins we beg,
    We bow to you with sorrow deep
Resolved to turn away from sin.
    That you our souls in grace may keep.**

**Almighty Father, hear our cry,
    Through Jesus Christ, our Lord most high,
Whom in the Spirit we adore,
    Who reigns with you forevermore. Amen.**

# ■ Intercessions

Leader: Jesus Christ, the new Adam, was obedient to his Father's will and accepted death on a cross. In his name, let us pray for:

Our Church
Our World
Our Nation
Our Community
Ourselves

Let us ask God to forgive our sins and to bring us to forgive those who sin against us:

**All:    Our Father ....**

## ■ Prayer

By the leader or by all:

> Merciful God,
> we are sinners like Adam and Eve,
> our first parents,
> but we are also your forgiven children,
> saved through the dying and rising of Jesus.
> Help us to be more like him in word and deed,
> so that we may give you glory
> in company with him.
> We ask this through the same Christ our Lord. Amen.

## ■ Blessing

Leader: May the only Son of God have mercy on us and help us in all our needs.

**All:**     **Amen.**

A sign of peace may be exchanged.

# Saturday Morning

Leader: How wonderful are your works, O Lord!

**All:** **In wisdom you have made them all!**

Leader: All praise be yours, O Lord, through everything that you have made.

**All:** **Glory and praise for ever!**

The Storyteller reads Genesis 1:31—2:3:

> God saw everything that he had made, and indeed, it was very good. And there was evening and there was morning, the sixth day.
>
> Thus the heavens and the earth were finished, and all their multitude. And on the seventh day God finished the work that he had done, and he rested on the seventh day from all the work that he had done. So God blessed the seventh day and hallowed it, because on it God rested from all the work that he had done in creation.

## ■ Psalm 104:24, 27–34, 35b
### Canticle of the Three Young Men (Dan 3:82,85,86,87)

Solo: God, how fertile your genius!
You shape each thing,
you fill the world
with what you do.

**All:** **All look to you for food
when they hunger;
you provide it and they feed.
You open your hand, they feast;
you turn away, they fear.**

Solo: You steal their breath,
they drop back into dust.
Breathe into them, they rise;
the face of the earth comes alive!

All: **Let God's glory endure
and the Lord delight in creating.
One look from God, earth quivers;
one touch, and mountains erupt.**

Solo: I will sing to my God,
make music for the Lord
as long as I live.
Let my song give joy to God
who is a joy to me.

All: **I will bless you, Lord!
Halleluia!** [*during Lent:* **Praise the Lord!**]

Solo: Bless God, children of earth.

All: **Give praise and glory.**

Solo: Bless God, servants of God.

All: **Give praise and glory.**

Solo: Bless God, just and faithful souls.

All: **Give praise and glory.**

Solo: Bless God, holy and humble hearts.

All: **Give praise and glory.**

All: **Glory to the Father, and to the Son,
and to the Holy Spirit:
as it was in the beginning, is now,
and will be for ever. Amen.**

# ■ Scripture Reading: Sirach 43:27–33

Reader: A reading from the Book of Sirach.

We could say more but could never say enough; let the final word be: "He is the all." Where can we find the strength to praise him? For he is greater than all his works. Awesome is the Lord and very great, and marvelous is his power. Glorify the Lord and exalt him as much as you can, for he surpasses even that. When you exalt him, summon all your strength, and do not grow weary, for you cannot praise him enough. Who has seen him and can describe him? Or who can extol him as he is? Many things greater than these lie hidden, for I have seen but few of his works. For the Lord has made all things, and to the godly he has given wisdom.

The word of the Lord.

**All:**     **Thanks be to God.**

# ■ Silent Reflection

# ■ Response to the Reading

**All:**     **Praise to our God, creation's Lord,**
          **Giver of gifts that fill our land,**
     **All living things with us accord:**
          **In love we know God's open hand.**

     **Praise to our God for flow of time:**
          **Journeys of sun and moon above,**
     **Season to season joy sublime:**
          **In these we mark our God's great love.**

     **Almighty Father, hear our cry,**
          **Through Jesus Christ, our Lord most high,**
     **Whom in the Spirit we adore,**
          **Who reigns with you forevermore. Amen.**

# ■ Intercessions

Leader: Let us bring before our God the needs of this day as we pray for:

> Our Family
> Our Neighbors
> Our Friends
> Our Parishioners
> Our Sisters and Brothers of the World

> Let us give glory to the God who makes holy our work and rest:

**All:** **Our Father ....**

# ■ Prayer

By the leader or by all:

> Good, very good,
> is your love, O Lord,
> that brings our world to life again
> each morning.
> Let us share your joy
> in all that you have made,
> and help us to live in this world
> with respect for all life.
> We ask this through Christ our Lord. Amen.

# ■ Blessing

Leader: May the Holy Spirit of God always fill our hearts with love.

**All:** **Amen.**

A sign of peace may be exchanged.

# Saturday Evening

Leader: How wonderful are your works, O Lord!

**All:      In wisdom you have made them all!**

Leader: All praise be yours, O Lord, through work and rest.

**All:      Glory and praise for ever!**

The Preacher:

> From a letter of Saint Clement, bishop of Rome:
> The great Creator and Lord of the universe
> commanded all these things to be established in
> peace and harmony, in his goodness to all, and in
> overflowing measure to us who seek refuge in his
> mercies through our Lord Jesus Christ; to him be
> glory and majesty for ever and ever. Amen.

## ■ Psalm 148

Solo:    Praise the Lord!
         Across the heavens,
         from the heights,
         all you angels, heavenly beings,
         sing praise, sing praise!

**All:      Sun and moon, glittering stars,
         sing praise, sing praise.
         Highest heavens, rain clouds,
         sing praise, sing praise.**

Solo:    Praise God's name,
         whose word called you forth
         and fixed you in place for ever
         by eternal decree.

All: **Let there be praise**
**from depths of the earth,**
**from creatures of the deep.**

Solo: Fire and hail, snow and mist,
storms, winds,
mountains, hills,
fruit trees and cedars,
wild beasts and tame,
snakes and birds,

All: **princes, judges,**
**rulers, subjects,**
**men, women,**
**old and young,**
**praise, praise the holy name,**
**this name beyond all names.**

Solo: God's splendor above the earth,
above the heavens,
gives strength to the nation,
glory to the faithful,
a people close to the Lord.
Israel, let there be praise!

All: **Glory to the Father, and to the Son,**
**and to the Holy Spirit:**
**as it was in the beginning, is now,**
**and will be for ever. Amen.**

## ■ Scripture Reading: Romans 11:33–36

Reader: A reading from the Letter of Saint Paul to
the Romans.

O the depth of the riches and wisdom and
knowledge of God! How unsearchable are his
judgments and how inscrutable his ways!

"For who has known the mind of the Lord? Or who
has been his counselor?"

"Or who has given a gift to him, to receive a gift in return?"

For from him and through him and to him are all things. To him be glory forever. Amen.

The word of the Lord.

**All:** **Thanks be to God.**

# ■ Silent Reflection

# ■ Response to the Reading

**All:** **Praise to our God for human life;**
**Parents and children, young and old,**
**People of peace instead of strife:**
**In these we see God's grace unfold.**

**Praise to our God, all-holy One:**
**Forever blessing, ever blest,**
**In worship true, in justice done,**
**May our whole lives God's gifts attest.**

**Almighty Father, hear our cry,**
**Through Jesus Christ, our Lord most high,**
**Whom in the Spirit we adore,**
**Who reigns with you forevermore. Amen.**

# ■ Intercessions

Leader: Let us pray to our God, the source, guide, and goal of all that is, as we remember:

Our Church
Our World
Our Nation
Our Community
Ourselves

Let us pray to our Creator as Jesus taught us:

**All:**    **Our Father ....**

## ■ Prayer

By the leader or by all:

> In doing our work,
> in taking our rest,
> in preparing to celebrate the Lord's Day,
> we ask your help, O God.
> Let all creation serve you
> and give you glory.
> Blest are you, O God,
> for beauty we have seen
> and for wonders still to come,
> through Jesus Christ, our Lord. Amen.

## ■ Blessing

Leader:   May almighty God bless us, the Father, the Son, and the Holy Spirit.

**All:**    **Amen.**

A sign of peace may be exchanged.

This book is available in bulk quantities.
For more information please contact:

Resource Publications, Inc.
160 E. Virginia St. #290
San Jose, CA 95112-5876
408-286-8505, 1-888-273-7782
Fax: 408-287-8748
info@rpinet.com, www.rpinet.com